THE
Archive Photographs
SERIES
AROUND
SPONDON

SPONDON LANE END, 1920. On arrival by train, this would be the first sight of the real Spondon a visitor would see on walking up Station Road, on the left. If visiting the main part of the village, he or she would have to face the stiff climb up the hill, past the thatched cottage. Spondon was about to witness a new phase in its development. The houses on the left along Derby Road were only three years old and within a few years the thatched cottage would be demolished. The growth of Spondon was beginning.

THE
Archive Photographs
SERIES

AROUND
SPONDON

Compiled by
John R. Hughes
for
Spondon Historical Society

CHALFORD

First published 1997
Copyright © John R. Hughes, 1997

The Chalford Publishing Company
St Mary's Mill, Chalford,
Stroud, Gloucestershire, GL6 8NX

ISBN 0 7524 0617 5

Typesetting and origination by
The Chalford Publishing Company
Printed in Great Britain by
Bailey Print, Dursley, Gloucestershire

Acknowledgements

The author wishes to thank the many people and organizations who have contributed to the production of this book, including:

BBC Radio Derby; Mrs Joyce Beardsmore of Spondon; Mr Dave Bennett, Derbyshire County Scout Camp Site Warden, Little Eaton; Mr Gerry Bentley of Chaddesden; Mr David Brown of Chaddesden; Mrs Molly Brown of Chaddesden; Mrs D.A. Clarke of Spondon (for permission to use Mr Winder's drawings); Courtaulds Chemicals of Spondon; Mr and Mrs C.R. Dean of Castle Donington; *Derby Evening Telegraph*; Mrs Lesley Gaskin of Chaddesden; Mrs Margaret Giller of Little Eaton; Mr B. Glasgow of Chaddesden; Mr and Mrs Paul Green of Stanley; Mrs M. Hall of Allestree; Mrs E. Hesketh of Chaddesden; Mr Charles Hurd of Breadsall; Miss Prudence Lewty of Frankston, Victoria, Australia; Mr and Mrs Moreton of Chaddesden; Mr W.J. Perry of Chaddesden; Mr and Mrs John Sibson of Breadsall; Spondon Historical Society; Miss Pam Stevens of Spondon; Mrs Jane Stewart of Mussleburgh, Scotland; Mrs Hilda Tillson of Spondon; Mr and Mrs Robert Thompson of Spondon; Mrs Rosemary Walsham of Spondon; Mrs P. Willson of Spondon; Miss Joyce Wright of Spondon and my wife, Mary.

Contents

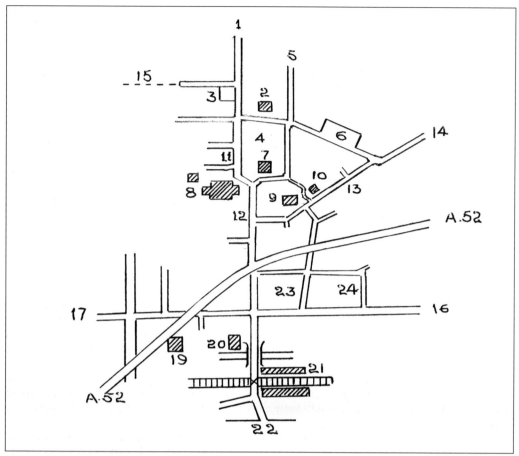

DIAGRAMMATIC PLAN OF SPONDON

(Not to scale)

1. Locko Road, to Locko, Stanley, Morley, Breadsall and Little Eaton
2. Village school
3. Spondon Cricket Ground
4. Site of Spondon House
5. Chapel Lane
6. Chapel Street and Chapel Side Precinct
7. Malt Shovel Inn, Potter Street
8. St Werburgh's church
9. The Homestead
10. Ingle Nook
11. Church Street
12. Church Hill
13. Sitwell Street
14. Moor Street and Dale Road, to Dale and Ockbrook
15. Footpath to Chaddesden
16. Nottingham Road, to Borrowash, Elvaston, Thulston, Shardlow and Wilne
17. Derby Road, to Chaddesden
18. Raynesway, to Alvaston
19. Site of Leech Neal Colour Works
20. Canal and Moon Hotel
21. Spondon station
22. Courtaulds Chemicals, formerly British Celanese, Ltd
23. Willowcroft Road
24. Cambridge Street

Introduction

East of the old Borough of Derby prior to 1900 lay a string of villages of varying sizes, many completely independent of the close proximity of the town, others relying on it in some way to provide employment or sources of income for their products. Like most larger towns and cities, Derby has grown over the years and especially so within the last thirty years, when expansion affected four of the villages covered by this book. Three of them, Chaddesden, Spondon and Alvaston, were completely outside the Borough until an act of 1901 incorporated sections within its boundary. All three were completely absorbed in an act of 1968. The fourth, Breadsall, lost an area of its farmland to the south of the village at the same time.

All of the villages featured here, except Borrowash and Wilne, existed before the Domesday Survey of 1086, when they were recorded for taxation purposes. At that time the villages were the property of various Norman magnates or William I himself.

The ancient village of Spondon possibly dates back to the time of the Roman evacuation of this area of Britain in about 390, when the Romano/Celtic people of Celtic origin who were left behind would want to get a little way away from the Roman-controlled settlement of Derventio, a part of Derby about three miles west. There is, however, no material evidence to prove this theory. The fact that there was settlement by the invading Angles, some time around the year 600 AD, is fairly certain. The word 'spon' probably comes from the old German for 'spoon', the oldest part of the village being in the spoon-shaped depression near the top of the hill. The 'don' indicates a village on a hill. A Roman road from Derventio to the River Trent at Sawley ran along what is now the old Derby to Nottingham road through the south side of the village.

The Domesday Survey gives some detail of the village, stating that it had a mill and a church, but its tax valuation was very low at five shillings and four pence. It had been owned by an Anglo-Saxon overlord named Stori, who, it appears, also held land and rights in Derby.

The manor of Spondon was granted to William de Ferrers, a favourite of William I, but a hundred years later his descendants had lost it by default and rebellion against the King. However, by then the de Ferrers had granted portions of land to the north of the village at Locko, plus the church itself, to the monastery of Burton Lazars, in Leicestershire. The monastery was run by a French order, the Knights of St Lazarus. The gift was confirmed by King John and the monastery continued to hold the church and some of its lands until the Dissolution of the Monasteries by Henry VIII. Part of the land at Locko was used by the Burton Lazars as a leper hospice for about 150 years from 1150 onwards. In contradiction to local belief, it was never used as a leper hospital in the modern sense of the word and was sited at Upper Locko. The present Locko Hall is in what used to be Nether Locko. The hospice probably never held more than a dozen lepers, many of whom paid for their care. There is a rumour that the hospice was burnt down, but there is no evidence to prove it.

A drastic fire in 1340 almost entirely burnt out Spondon village, destroying the church and all but four houses. Old records state that a woman was drying malt before the fire in the malting-house during a strong east wind. The fire blew back, ignited the floor and very soon the whole village was ablaze. The church lost all the vestments, library, tower and bells. One villager, Henry Penk, lost his life in the catastrophe. Edward III granted the village freedom of taxes for one year. The village and the church were rebuilt and the church was completed around the year 1390. Much of the existing church, including the chancel, south wall of the nave and the tower, date back to this rebuild.

The church is dedicated to the Anglo-Saxon Werburgh, a very popular princess, (daughter of a King of Mercia), who became a nun and later abbess to avoid being involved in any form of political marriage. As she died around 701 and was probably declared a saint very soon afterwards, this may give a clue as to the date of Spondon's first church.

Areas of Locko were sold by the monastery to the Byrd family before the Dissolution, who sold it to William Gilbert around 1590. They held Locko until 1747, apart from a break when the Hall was rebuilt, until the Lowes (later the Drury-Lowes) purchased it in 1747. In 1643 or 1644 St Werburgh's church suffered slight damage following a Civil War skirmish. The marks of musket ball shots can be seen on the north wall of the chancel, probably caused when a Royalist force came from the north of Derbyshire almost to Derby, in an attempt to clear the area of Parliamentarians. There is, however, no mention of this in the church records and the tradition is that Spondon, including the Gilberts of Locko, kept out of the conflict as much as possible.

Spondon continued as a quiet agricultural village until the nineteenth century, when industry began to take effect. At first the only industrial activity was stocking frame knitting, then nearby factories at Borrowash and Derby had an effect. In the late eighteenth century improved roads had made Spondon a desirable place to live and many professional people such as solicitors and factory owners began to have houses built. Most of the larger ones have now been demolished, but some of the smaller remain. By the 1850s the major source of employment was frame knitting or domestic service. The railway came to Spondon in 1839 and within twenty years men began to gain employment at the railway, either in the workshops of the Midland Railway or at stations and as train operatives.

In 1916 the British Cellulose and Chemical Manufacturing Company obtained land on the south side of the village, between the Derby and Nottingham Roads and the River Derwent. This area was farming land, thinly populated due to the danger of flooding. At first they produced an aircraft fabric strengthening product (cellulose, generally called 'dope'), but after the First World War started to make acetate yarn. The name changed to British Celanese, the product range expanded to knitting and weaving the yarn, other products were introduced, until it reached its height of employment after the Second World War. In 1957 British Celanese was taken over by the Courtaulds Group. The effect on the village by the expansion of the company, plus easier transport to the other main Derby factories, made a huge impact on the village population. In 1841, the population was given as approximately 1,600. By 1891 it had risen to 2,200 but by 1991 it was over 14,000.

Spondon remained an independent village until 1968, when it was incorporated into the Borough, now the City of Derby. Many of its inhabitants still encourage an independent life on the edge of the city, guarding its ever-decreasing 'green belt' from encroachment.

On approaching Spondon, the one prominent building is the church, standing on the top of the hill and with its tower dominating the skyline, as it has done since around 1390. It would seem appropriate, therefore, to include Spondon's oldest structure as a section in this book.

Chaddesden and Stanley were at one time chapelries of Spondon but by 1345, Chaddesden had gained some independence. The villagers of Chaddesden complained that they were unable to carry their dead to Spondon for burial when the Lees Brook flooded, so they were granted permission to have their own burial site at their church. One factor in their favour was also probably the fact that Spondon's church had been burnt down five years earlier. The footpath between Chaddesden and Spondon churches, the old 'coffin track', still exists. However, the permission given to Chaddesden was on the agreement that the Vicar of Spondon still received the burial fees. Stanley continued as a chapelry until early in the nineteenth century. Again, the old track between Spondon and Stanley still remains as a public footpath, passing through the parkland of Locko, although a little diverted in one area. The old paths between all the various villages also remain, many still just footpaths, although some have inevitably become roads, but there is still no direct road between Spondon and Chaddesden, Ockbrook or Stanley.

No doubt the villages will continue to grow, despite the efforts of the many who want to retain some semblance of village life. It is, however, hoped that in years to come enough remains for people to be able to say 'it still looks as it did a hundred years ago'.

One

Spondon at School

There are references to the start of a village school in Spondon in 1662, initially a 'grammar school', but it only lasted until 1669. Before the end of the century however, another school had commenced and this was the true foundation of a more or less continuous village school system. A stone lintel from this early village school still exists, dated 1699, with the motto Ingredere ut Proficias, although the school itself was demolished in the 1950s, having become redundant in 1839.

SPONDON SCHOOL, c. 1900. The village school in Chapel Street opened in 1839 and was enlarged in 1887. The Headmaster, Mr D.G. Douglas, who held the post from 1867 to 1906, was a much-loved man who worked hard for both school and village. Even after his retirement he continued to work in a voluntary capacity for the good of Spondon. Here he is with thirty of his boys, probably from two classes, all looking very smart for the photograph, outside the school.

CLASS OF SIX. A group of boys who attended the Church of England School in Chapel Street, in about 1897. All looking extremely smart, the group had probably received an award, presented by the unnamed, seated gentleman. He was not a member of the school staff, as the only male member was Mr Douglas, who had a large beard. The only boy who can be identified is George Wright, the taller of the two boys at the back.

THE INFANTS, c. 1900. By 1900 the school had over 300 pupils, including more than 100 infants, in a building with 6 classrooms and a large hall. Here we see 24 boys and 37 girls, with, it appears, more 'lost' off the left edge of the picture. They are all members of the infants section and the lady teacher on the right is one of the 5 lady members of staff: Miss Georgina Smith, Miss Fancourt, Miss Hammerton, Miss Roberts and Miss M.A. Smith. Miss Georgina Smith was the Girl's Mistress, presumably, therefore, senior to the other lady members of staff, so it is probable that she is the lady featured.

SCHOOL CHAMPIONS. The village school soccer team, schools' league champions of 1910/11, with the Headmaster Mr Thomas Creighton, proudly display their trophy. The team, from left to right, standing: Jos. Twigg, L. Stevens, L. Wheatley, Jos. Murfin, Frank Coxon, Sid Ward and Bill Peat. Seated: Ken Riley, Fred Litchfield, Eric Maddocks and John Painter. The school was in Chapel Street and later became the village junior school.

PREP. SCHOOL SCOUTS. In 1908 Spondon House Preparatory School formed one of the first Scout Troops in Derbyshire. The Deputy Master, Mr F.H. Lewes, commenced the troop almost as soon as the weekly issues of *Scouting for Boys* was published. It was later registered as the 3rd Derby Troop. Two patrols, complete with bugler, are seen training on the school sports ground.

HOSPITAL STAFF. Spondon House was requisitioned as an Auxiliary Hospital during the First World War. The staff of the Derby No. 14 Voluntary Aid Detachment were formed and based at the house and are here seen when it was opened as a hospital in November 1914. Seated left of the Chief Medical Officer is the Commandant, Mrs M. Lewty, of Ingle Nook in Sitwell Street. The only other person definitely identified is Mrs A. Wright of Spondon, on the extreme right of the back row.

SPONDON HOUSE. Built in about 1790 by
the Drury-Lowe family of Locko Park, it was
only used by a member of the family for a
short time. In the early 1800s it became a
'School for Young Ladies', then from 1860 to
1913 a preparatory school for boys. The print
was taken from a lino-cut made for the 1930
edition of the Spondon House school
magazine *Avanti*, by Mr R. Elliott, an art
master at the school. It is typical of the
artistic style of the period.

SPONDON HOUSE STAFF. In 1922 Spondon School's senior section officially moved to
Spondon House, although many of them were already using the premises, by arrangement with
the owner, Mr J.F.A. Drury-Lowe of Locko Park. The Derbyshire Education Authority then
purchased the property. The staff in 1922 are not named, except that sitting in the centre is the
Headmaster, Mr Thomas Creighton. It had been his aim for many years to move into Spondon
House.

CLASS OF '46. In the late 1920s there was a growing need for more junior school accommodation and so in 1932 the new Springfield School was opened on West Road. Here is Mrs Burrow's class in September 1946 and we are lucky to have the names of almost every member. Back row, from left to right: Roger Borrington, -?-, Tony Young, David Young, John Stewart, Kenneth Bennett, Bernard Richardson, Jimmy Tunnicliffe, Ronald Slater, Neil Arbon, Mrs Burrows. Centre row: Malcolm ?, Robert Mee, John North, Beryl Wickens, June Slater, Monica Brown, Gladys Simpson, Tony Howard, -?-, John Brentnall, Terry Livesey. Front row: Joy Travis, Hannah Topliss, -?-, Margaret Davey, Joan Thrupp, Kathleen Vickers, Margaret Curzon, Lesley Meakin, Gillian Roberts, Marion Slater, Rosemary Chilton, Maureen Leahy.

Two
Spondon Church Life

From the earliest days St Werburgh's church played a large part in the life of the inhabitants of Spondon. Today four religious groups serve the needs of the village - the Church of England, the Methodist church, the Free Church and Jehovah's Witnesses, whilst the nearby village of Borrowash has a relatively new Roman Catholic church.

ST WERBURGH'S CHURCH, c. 1830. In 1826 a considerable restoration took place in the church, although the south and east exterior walls and the tower remained unaltered. The pitch of the roof was lowered and the north side was rebuilt to a rather unfortunate design. By 1896 it was again altered, more to the original design. This aspect gives a fairly good idea of what the early rebuild of 1826 looked like externally.

THE CHURCH INTERIOR, *c.* 1904. Unfortunately there is no picture of the interior prior to the 1894-1896 alterations, when the church had box pews and galleries. Here the church is illuminated by oil lamps and candles. It was not until 1908 that gas lighting was installed and electricity did not follow until the 1920s. Apart from the lighting, the only difference today is the removal of the ornate altar hangings and the curtains at the east wall, behind the altar.

ST WERBURGH'S CHURCH, *c.* 1910. This scene is almost unchanged today, except for the trimming back of some of the trees and a different lamp post. The main feature is the north porch, erected some fourteen years earlier. On the extreme right, partly obscured by the trees, is Church Cottage, believed to be the one mentioned in a deed of the mid-sixteenth century.

ST WERBURGH'S CHURCH,
c. 1930. Viewed from the junction of
Church Hill and Potter Street and the
remains of the original green, is the
north east side of the church, showing
the 1896 rebuild of this side. The
object behind the post box is an
electricity junction box, which stood
for many years on the edge of the
green. There have been no burials in
the churchyard since the 1920s and the
gravestones have now been moved to
sites around the outer walls.

MEMORIAL SERVICE FOR QUEEN
VICTORIA, 1901. Spondon mourned
the death of Queen Victoria, the only
ruler of the nation that the vast majority
of parishioners could remember. The
service was in January or February and
there are traces of snow around as the
congregation queue to enter the church.
Note the flags at half mast on both the
church tower and the pole of Church
Cottage at the side of the church path.

ST WERBURGH'S, *c.* 1930. A lino-cut by pupil Robert Thompson from the school magazine *Avanti* of Spondon's parish church. An earlier church was burnt down in 1340 when a disastrous fire burnt out almost the entire village and completely destroyed the church. Robert Thompson, Bob as he is generally known, still lives in the village with his wide Cecilia, who contributed to the magazine with an article giving the history of Spondon House.

THE ALTAR, *c.* 1950. The new form of service, which commenced in the 1980s, included the moving of the altar away from the east wall, which also meant that the hangings could not be used. Prior to this sets of hangings were made for the various church seasons. It is believed that this set was prepared and presented by Mrs Keating of Lodge Lane in the 1950s and photographed by a former church member, Miss Gwenyth Nichols.

THE OLD VICARAGE. This is a fine building with part dating back to the mid-seventeenth century. Since then it has been enlarged on several occasions, the last being in 1815, when the present east frontage was completed. The building is now a residential home and has been sympathetically enlarged and altered, although the depicted south east section remains unaltered.

SUNDAY SCHOOL EVENT, *c.* 1926. This was an unknown event, but apparently held on behalf of the church Sunday school. The only people who can be identified with certainty are the Revd H.C. Brocklehurst, who had been appointed in 1925, local teacher Mrs L. Nichols, (née Rice) on the extreme left, and Arthur Croxall, the third young man from the left on the back row. Judging from the front row, it appears to be an occasion when hats were required.

THE BOYS' AND MEN'S CHOIR, *c.* 1930. Seen in the extensive grounds of the Old Vicarage are, back row, from left to right: Mr Disney, Mr Weatherburn, Mr F. Williams, Mr Spencer, Mr Chawner, Mr Beniston, Mr C. Sims, Mr Coxon, -?-, Mr J. Laing, Mr S. Coxon, Mr A. Walker. Middle row: -?-, Mr Brighouse, Revd H.C. Brocklehurst (vicar), Mr A. Berriman, Mr J. Cooper. Front row: ? Hibbert, Peter Thompson, Fred Berriman, Harry Lacey, Leslie Cope, Bob Thompson, Tom Cooper.

MEN'S BIBLE CLASS, 1936. Sir Henry Fowler, leader, with members of the Spondon Young Men's Bible Class, which had been in existence since 1902, but finally closed during the Second World War. The group is outside St Werburgh's Church Institute, more commonly known to Spondonians over many years as 'the Iron Room' due to its corrugated steel sheeting construction. The building was finally demolished in 1995.

SUNDAY SCHOOL PARADE. The St Werburgh's Sunday school banner in the annual Whit Sunday Parade in about 1935. It stood over 12 ft high and was difficult to control in a wind, despite two strong men to carry the poles plus four people on the guy ropes. It was used until the 1960s then, after storage in the Old Vicarage for some years, it could not be found.

THE GIRLS' FRIENDLY SOCIETY, *c.* 1936. Spondon St Werburgh's Girls' Friendly Society outside Locko Hall at a party given by Mrs Dorothy Drury-Lowe, to celebrate the winning of the Derbyshire GFS shield. Mrs F. Paynter is holding the shield and the lady in the hat standing next to her is Mrs Drury-Lowe. On the left of the back row is Mrs Hervy, the wife of the curate of St Werburgh's at that time.

Three

Spondon at Leisure

Being a medium-sized village, it has only been in recent years that Spondon has looked beyond its boundaries to find leisure interests, from football, cricket and going to the pub, to Scouts, Guides, Women's Institutes, Mother's Union and numerous similar organizations. Lacking a true Village Hall until the 1950s, meetings took place in a variety of locations.

THE WHITE SWAN, *c.* 1870. An early eighteenth century inn, it was run by a member of the Coxon family for over one hundred years. It faces down Sitwell Street, in front of which is a busy road junction. It still has the steps and retaining wall to the main door. Until about forty years ago, the Meynell Hunt would meet outside the inn before setting off to hunt the area around Locko, a mile or so north of the village.

MALT SHOVEL INN, *c.* 1949. The section of the inn at right angles to the main building, seen on the left, is early eighteenth century and recent excavations to check the foundations revealed that it stands on the stone base of an earlier structure. Potter Street is considered to be the oldest street in the village, so it is not unlikely that a succession of inns have stood on this spot.

MALT SHOVEL INN, POTTER STREET, *c.* 1945. Traditionally, the site is the start of a disastrous fire of 1340 which completely destroyed the village, including the church, leaving only four houses standing. The drawing, by the late Mr R. Winder, shows a building with a timber front on the right which was to be demolished shortly afterwards. Some internal parts of the building are said by experts to date from the sixteenth century.

SPONDON CYCLING CLUB. 'A celebration run' is the only descriptive information that is available. Approximately twenty-five members, including seven very elegant-looking ladies, are setting out some time around 1910, possibly to celebrate the coronation of George V. To protect those long skirts the ladies' cycles had a metal case enclosing the chains, and usually a mesh covering around the rear wheel and mudguard.

SPONDON IVANHOE FC. This was the first team from the season 1908/9, in the Long Eaton and District League. Only the team plus the trainer are named, the others being reserves, committee and the like. Third row from front: Mr A. Cotton (trainer, with towel), George Wright, E. Frost (goalkeeper), W. Hay (vice-captain). Second row: F. Stone, F. Oldershaw (captain), William Dally. Front row: Sam Auckland, D. Fletcher, Harry Holmes (secretary), W. Hibbs, George Hay. No team squad in those days - the same team played each week unless someone was injured or their play was bad enough for them to be dropped. The normal form of transport to away matches was on the horse drawn wagon of Mr Richard Dedman.

SPONDON FC, *c.* 1912. What appears to be an *ad hoc* football team on the playing field of the 'Spondon House School for the Sons of Gentlemen'. The team consists of masters from the school, some local players and one or two introduced friends who were members of the famous Corinthians team from the Oxford and Cambridge Universities. It played occasional matches and was captained by Mr James Lewty, of Ingle Nook.

SPONDON ROVERS FOOTBALL CLUB, 1929. At Derby County's Baseball Ground for the final of a local cup competition, in the days when a team consisted of a regular eleven players and no substitutes are, back row, from left to right: F. Litchfield, F. Little, E. Maddocks, J. Coxon, T. Stevens and T. Coxon. Front row: L. Reader, E. Trigg, H. Caughey, G. Antill and G. Astill. The majority of the surnames can be traced through Spondon records for a hundred years or more.

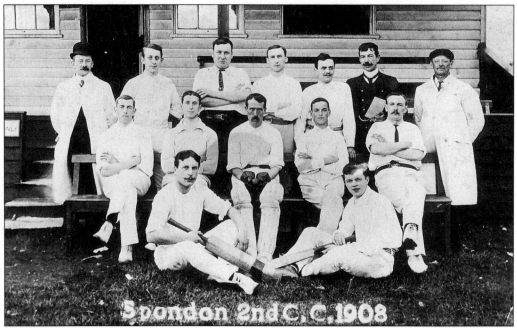

SPONDON CRICKET CLUB SECOND XI, 1908. The club has a very long history, reaching back over 100 years. Not all of the names are known, but second from the left on the back row is Arthur Thompson and the scorer is Tom Antill. The three in the centre of the seated row are, from left to right: Mr Meakin, Harry Wilford and Jack Porter. On the ground, left, is George Antill.

SPONDON CRICKET CLUB, c. 1910. A small, informal group of members of Spondon Cricket Club, including second from left, T.C. Hayman and fourth, Bill Thompson. T.C. Hayman, who came to Spondon Preparatory School for boys in the 1890s, was the Headmaster from 1907 until 1913. He was an enthusiastic and very good cricketer, playing for the village team for most of his time in Spondon.

SPONDON FIRST XI, c. 1912. Outside their pavilion off Royal Hill Road, are, back row, from left to right: -?-, ? Walker, Jack Porter, Arthur Thompson, -?-. Seated: Alf Cope, George Porter, Henry Fowler, Bill Thompson, Ken Cameron. Front row: Ted Frost, Stan Rose, Jack Dally. Henry Fowler, the team captain, was Chief Engineer on the old Midland Railway and later knighted for his services to railway engineering. Over the years, several of Spondon's players have also played for Derbyshire.

SPONDON FIRST XI, c. 1928. Another trophy for Spondon. Back row, from left to right: Tant Moyle, Sam Murfin, Frank Watts, Tom Wilson, Mac Smith, Eric Walker, Jack Dally and Percy Borrington. Front row: Walter Porter, Jim Sinfoil, R.H. Finney, L. Latham, Tom Stevens, Tony Ward and Charles Hastings. The club played in the Notts and Derby Border League, now called the Derbyshire County League.

SPONDON NATIONAL FIRE SERVICE CREW. In wartime, 'leisure' activities mainly consisted of doing voluntary work. In addition to their normal daytime (or shift) jobs, Spondon people gave up much of their time to doing voluntary work of varying kinds. A fire service base was established in Sitwell Street and here the 1943 crew display their efficiency awards. The crew are, back row, from left to right: T. Sadler, ? Young, L/F Richard Cape, Jim Crooks, David Dalrymple. Centre row: Frank Cape, L/F Arthur Pollard, ? Ashworth, ? Smith, L. Pearce, ? Thornber, ? Rivers, L/F Weaver. Front row: Hilda Cockayne, Minnie Jackson, Company Officer D. Raynor, Doris Grundy, B. Waite. The three cups are for Division, Area, and Region large trailer pump drill.

SPONDON 'A' FLIGHT, 2069 SQUADRON, AIR TRAINING CORPS. Many young men of pre-National Service age joined the ATC, the local flight meeting at the 'Iron Room' at the rear of the playground of the Church of England (St. Werburgh's) School in Chapel Street. Not all of the members have been identified, but so far as records are available, they are, back row, from left to right: -?-, Bill Slater, Douglas Whitmore, Alan Hitchcock, Peter Auckland, Andrew Hall, Alan Birbeck, -?-, Ted Godson. Middle row: Bill Hibbert, Bill Slater, Bob Rivers, C/O Alec Ward, Bill Godson, -?-. Front row: Harry Gillingham, Gordon Chambers. Mr Alec Ward worked at the British Celanese works in Spondon. The Flight proudly display the trophies gained at an 'away' base, presumably 'somewhere in the Midlands'.

SPONDON GUIDES, 1958. In camp at Locko Park is 1st Spondon Guide Company Captain Mrs Joyce Wright (front left), with her assistant Miss Copestake (centre), keeping an eye on the cooking achievements of Guides Olivia Hughes (rear left) and Liz Davies. A Guiding or Scouting examiner would very soon point out the failings of their camp kitchen layout, as no doubt did their leaders!

SPONDON SCOUT HQ, c. 1968. In 1935 the Spondon Scouts, (66th Derby), purchased a disused one hundred year old Primitive Methodist chapel in Gladstone Street as their first permanent headquarters. The apex of this building can be seen behind an extension, built in 1966 and facing onto Moor Street. By 1975 the group had moved to a new headquarters and this building was sold for industrial purposes. It was eventually knocked down and two new houses have been erected on the site.

SPONDON SCOUTS PARTY, c. 1930. This is rather a mystery event, because although we know that the occasion was a party given by Spondon Scouts and Rovers to the members of the St Werburgh's church Girls' Friendly Society, we are not certain as to the purpose. It was held in the old Mission Hall in Stoney Lane, which was knocked down some fifty years later. Why are the Scouts in full uniform, when nearly all the members of the GFS are in fancy dress?

Four

Spondon Village Streets

Probably until the mid-eighteenth century the layout of the village changed very little, with the centre in Potter Street and around the church. Over the last 250 years the centre has gradually grown outwards and now, sights and locations which were familiar only a hundred years ago have changed, sometimes beyond recognition. Over this last hundred years, perhaps the streets which have changed most have been Church Street, Chapel Street and Sitwell Street.

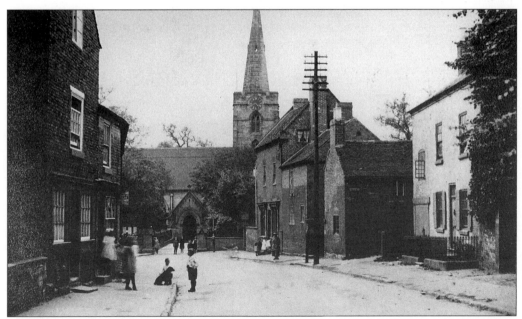

CHURCH STREET, *c.* 1910. With the exception of the church, all the properties shown have now been demolished. On the right nearest the church was the bakery of Mr John Craddock; to the right of the telegraph pole was a row of cottages called The Alley and the house on the extreme right, No. 6 Church Street, was the home of Mr and Mrs William Randle. Mr Randle was a churchwarden of St Werburgh's church in 1918 and 1919.

CHURCH STREET, *c.* 1940. On the left is the stables entrance to Spondon House, which for the previous twenty years had been Spondon House County School. The wall and this entrance still exists. On the right are the farm buildings and house of Church Farm. The house remains, but the farm buildings were demolished in the 1960s and are now the site of two houses. Beyond Church Farm is the corner of the wall of The Grove, an already demolished early nineteenth century dwelling.

CHURCH HILL, *c.* 1930. On the right is The Old Farm and at the top of the hill, Church Hill Terrace. Church Hill was cut through the steep hillside in about 1815 as a continuation to Lodge Lane - now, after the intersection by the A52, Lodge Lane North. Even after cutting, the road was too much for some horses and a spring, now dried up, fed into a trough in the churchyard wall to give a much-needed drink.

CHURCH HILL TERRACE, c. 1910. Built on the site of the old village green in the eighteenth and nineteenth centuries, it was an early village shopping centre. The triangle of grass in the foreground was all that remained of the green. The tree in the front was planted to commemorate the Diamond Jubilee of Queen Victoria. The passage to the right was called Post Office Yard, the earliest post office being located here. All the buildings were demolished in the early 1960s. Blocks of low level flats cover the area, still following the triangular site plan.

THE OLD FARM. Built on Church Hill shortly after the road was cut through, it is now no longer a farm but still retains the farmyard at the rear, with the entrance through the doors on the left. This is a good indication of the amount of earth cut away to make the road. The photographer was standing in the churchyard, which is still at the original ground level and a considerable height above the road.

CHURCH HILL, 1985. The Old Farm is on the left, stretching down Church Hill to Lodge Lane and Sitwell Street. The original farmhouse is in the centre, with a slightly later extension - most likely to an existing building - to the right. On the corner and now still part of the house was the old threshing barn; some records name the farm as Threshing Barn Farm. It was said to be a very noisy corner when threshing was in progress.

36

CHURCH HILL TERRACE CORNER, 1949. This is another of Mr Winder's drawings. The old confectionary shop 'up the steps' was run by Miss Marsden. Hundreds of former Spondon House School pupils will remember it, with the occasional visit on their way into or out of school. On the left the shops round the corner into Church Street included a gents' hairdresser, a greengrocer and a butcher. The greengrocer always seemed to have a large cat snoozing in the middle of the window.

CHAPEL STREET, 1905. Prominent on the right is the Co-operative store, then the Co-op butchery and beyond that the manager's house, now a Balti restaurant, an Indian takeaway and a children's nursery respectively. The first two of the three identical houses lower down the road still exist; beyond them now are shops, flats and a medical centre. On the left is the original wall of Beech House and farm, together with the first cottages below it, all now demolished.

CHAPEL STREET, *c.* early 1914. The same street in the opposite direction, viewed from almost the same position. On the immediate left is the post office which had then only recently moved from Church Hill. The entrance to Chapel Lane is on the right and the bell tower of the village school can be seen to the right of the trees. Bowes House is prominent on the right and all the property is still in existence today.

BEECH HOUSE. The Barton family farmhouse in Chapel Street, it was demolished around 1970 when the Chapel Side Precinct was built. The house was named after the beech tree which stood in front of it. In the foreground can be seen the walls of some of the old farm workers' cottages. The fronts were retained to act as a wall. It is said that they were quite unique as farm cottages, their layout being detailed and sent to London for record before their demolition.

BARTON'S FARMYARD. Note the elaborate design of the ventilation brickwork in the walls of the stable, being used as a chicken pen and store. At the right edge of the picture is the side of Beech House, shown in the preceding photograph. The Barton family were well known as farmers and butchers for many years, with a shop at the corner of Sitwell Street and Chapel Street.

CHAPEL LANE, c. 1912. Running from Chapel Street is a very old track, named Chapel Lane when names became necessary, although the cottages were built around the mid-nineteenth century, some time before this was a requirement. Just beyond the cottages the lane was gated, but it was a popular walk for local villagers. Unfortunately we do not know the names of the family pictured.

CHAPEL LANE, *c.* 1920. Three friends having a chat at one of the cottages. No more houses were built in the lane until the 1930s and, until the 1950s, the lane was not a through road. The motor cycle and sidecar in the hedge were probably the property of one of the residents, parked out of the way of farm vehicles going along the road to the fields beyond.

LOCKO ROAD, *c.* 1935. The outbuilding on the left, formerly the joiner's workshop of Mr Thompson, was later demolished and houses were built where the overgrown hedge grew. A pedestrian entrance to the nearly one hundred year old Spondon Cricket Ground now exists at the opening on the extreme left. The road includes houses ranging from the late eighteenth century to the 1980s.

FRESH FIELDS. Instead of walking along Locko Road to Locko, villagers have for over two hundred years taken a path off Longley Lane, down Royal Hill to this beautiful pasture land of wild flowers and ancient trees. The path goes back to the days of the Enclosure Acts when Locko Road was moved at the approach to Locko Park and villagers made a path to cut off the new bend and corner.

HALL DYKE, c. 1920. A group of three cottages built on a curve (which created unusual room shapes) at the junction of Potter Street. The cottages and almost all of the wall were knocked down in the 1950s. One of the cottages was once the home of George Porter, chimney sweep and well known fast bowler for Derbyshire. Hall Dyke is part of an ancient track running from Spondon to Locko.

SITWELL STREET, c. 1920. The main item soon to disappear is the old smithy, the lean-to building reaching the roadside on the right. It was still very much in use at this time and a horse drawn hay-rake is outside waiting for repair. At approximately the point in the road where the two men stand talking, is now a pedestrian operated set of traffic lights to halt the flow of traffic so that people can cross in safety.

SITWELL STREET, c. 1930. In the left foreground is The Wilderness, part of which some will remember as the surgery of Dr Rudge. It is now the site of a supermarket. The trees obscure the shops leading to Chapel Street, and Poplar Avenue had not been built. The lower section of wall beyond the road sign was demolished and the avenue, plus three shops in Sitwell Street, were constructed approximately three years later.

SITWELL STREET, *c. 1950.* How many Spondonians still remember buying ice cream from the kiosk outside Alan Steven's shop to the left of the parked car? The delicious ice cream was made in a dairy at the rear of the shop. Ice cream sales ceased in the 1960s but the shop remains. The row of cottages in the right foreground, which included Coxon's butchers, was demolished to make way for a supermarket, now a car accessories business, plus other smaller shops. The first of the buildings which still remains is now a hardware store.

REAR OF SITWELL STREET. From what is now the Recreation Ground, this view looks on the backs of some of the houses on the south side of the street. The ivy-clad house in the centre was the home and the shop of Mr Housley, the dispensing chemist. South Avenue, which had not been built, was a lane beyond the hedge in the foreground. The hollow is known as 'Joey's Pancheon'. The path from the east side of Mr Housley's is known as 'Rowney's Twitchell'.

WEST END OF SITWELL STREET. The street on a wet day in the early 1930s. The wall on the right is the boundary of The Homestead, and on the left is the farm of Mr Richard Dedman. The horse trough by the railings on the right side of the road was fed by a constant supply of water from one of Spondon's many springs until, in 1950, some nearby building work diverted the flow.

MOOR STREET. At the opposite end of Sitwell Street a bend in the road signifies the change of name to Moor Street, which is the road out of Spondon towards Ockbrook, Dale and Ilkeston. This is a fairly modern picture but without the traffic calming island which has been constructed outside the White Swan. As the name suggests, Moor Street leads to a much built-over Spondon Moor.

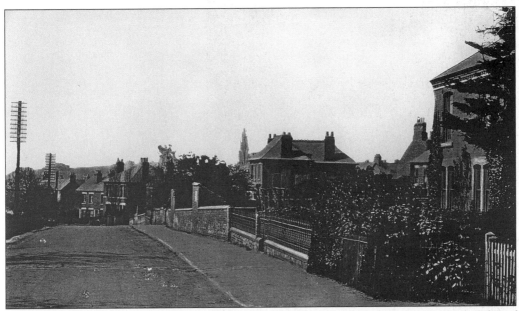

DALE ROAD, *c.* 1920. Moor Street originally led off to the right to the one-time hamlet of Moor End, with Dale Road taking over as the main road. The beginning of the road has mainly Victorian residences, but even here the gaps such as the one behind the brick wall have now been filled in with more modern houses. As the road proceeds to the Spondon and Derby City boundary, the development can be seen in the changes of house styles, right up to the 1980s.

SOUTH OF DALE ROAD, *c.* 1930. Until the late 1940s there was a stretch of farmland from Dale Road over to Ockbrook and almost down to the Nottingham Road. Taken from a window of a house in the road, looking south east, the only building in the middle distance is Coxon's farm. In the distance is the village of Borrowash and, to the right, the towers of Spondon Power Station.

SPONDON LANE END, *c.* 1936. This was the main Derby to Nottingham road until the building of the A52 in the late 1950s. The houses facing and continuing along the Derby Road were built in 1917-1918 by British Celanese Ltd, originally as houses for employees who were required to be near the factory site, which was beyond the station on the road to the left. The 'Teas and Refreshments' sign referred to Glover's shop on the corner, a one-time grocery and confectionary store, sub-post office and small cafe.

SPONDON LANE END, *c.* 1960. The same road junction but facing the opposite direction and looking down Nottingham Road. Glover's shop (see page 46) is on the extreme right. To many, the change of road name at this point, from Derby Road to Nottingham Road, creates confusion. One hundred years ago it was known throughout as The Turnpike. The houses on the left were built in the 1920s and 1930s.

THE THATCHED LODGE, *c.* 1910. The cottage was built towards the end of the eighteenth century as a lodge to Spondon Hall and was sited at the corner of Lodge Lane and Derby Road. Originally only the hall drive, Lodge Lane was extended into Spondon in about 1815. In the late nineteenth century the mails for Spondon were dropped here to avoid the mail cart having to be driven up the hill. The cottage was demolished in the 1920s to make way for a bank.

NOTTINGHAM ROAD, c. 1910. Most of this area, south of the original village, was built around 1880, mainly to house senior officials of the Midland Railway, who had their headquarters in Derby. It is relatively near Spondon station and employees were able to commute by train direct from Spondon to their place of work. The large house projecting forward in the centre is now a day nursery for young children.

NOTTINGHAM ROAD, c. 1930. The wall on the left is the frontage of what is now The Laurels Nursing Home. On the right is the wall and entrance to the drive of a large house, The Pastures, now demolished, Stoney Cross house, now The Crown pub, and Stoney Cross cottages. The trees on the right have all been removed. The houses on the left and the entrance to Cambridge Street remain unchanged.

Five
Spondon Celebrates

Like all other towns and villages, Spondon enjoys celebrating, especially when it commemorates a national event, although annual carnivals and parades create fun and enjoyment - and a lot of hard work for the organizers. Weddings, too, are cause for celebration, as well as being a most solemn occasion, so it is fitting to include such events.

SPONDON CARNIVAL. The 1st Spondon Brownie Pack preparing to set off with their entry for the Spondon Village Carnival in 1956. The two ladies 'disguised' as witches are Brownie Leaders Miss Mary Chapman and Mrs Stanley. The only two Brownies who can definitely be identified are Lesley Nichols (now Mrs Lesley Gaskin), who is second from the left in the standing centre group of four and Julie Wright, the first from the left in the kneeling group.

JUBILEE CELEBRATIONS. The Silver Jubilee of George V in 1935 brought out the crowds in the village, with everyone making for the space at the top of Church Hill. A brass band played nearby, windows were open and broadcast speeches were relayed to the crowd. Everyone put on their best clothes for the occasion, (note the man in the light suit with the 'Oxford bags' towards the left and the young lady in the foreground, right).

CORONATION PARTY. A street party to celebrate the Coronation of George VI in 1937, organized by the residents for the children of Oxford Street. The photograph was loaned by Miss Joyce Wright, who still lives in Oxford Street. Joyce is the rather serious-looking young girl third from the right at the rear of the picture, next to the two ladies. Space does not permit us to name the rest of the group.

CORONATION PARTY, SIXTEEN YEARS ON. The children (and adults) of Cambridge Street, at their party, celebrating the Coronation of Elizabeth II in 1953. Great efforts were made to give the street a festive air, but the wind played havoc with the bunting. At least two of the houses have rigged up temporary lights to brighten up the proceedings and it was unlikely that anyone went to bed at a normal time, with music and dancing going on outside and then indoors until, in some cases, the very early hours.

SHEEP ROAST. This was probably the main attraction also taking place in Church Hill. Sheep, already prepared and cut into sections, were roasted on spits before a specially constructed fire. It was obviously hot work, and the thirsty cooks needed plenty of liquid refreshment. It would be interesting to know what was in the jug!

CUTTING UP THE MUTTON. How long had the people been waiting, their mouths watering, for their mutton (or lamb) cob? Slicing the meat is Mr Billy Barton, a well known local butcher, whose family had by then been running a butchery business in Spondon for sixty-seven years. The business finally ceased connection with the family after a further fifty-eight years.

SPONDON CORONATION BAND, 1936. The band was formed to commemorate the Coronation of George VI and this is their first parade. It continued in existence for about fifty years, during which time they had at least three different styles of uniform. They travelled throughout England, competing in all the major carnival band contests and winning many of them, including on one occasion the the English National Championship.

'SPONDON AFLAME', 1990. To commemorate the 650th anniversary of the fire which virtually burnt out the whole of the village, six months of various events were held, including church services, a specially written musical and a medieval market, with street entertainers and the like. Three wandering minstrels play to the crowds as they make their way down Hall Dyke to Potter Street and the market.

WEDDING, *c*. 1900. The Spondon wedding of Miss Emily Wright to Mr Charles Carter. The bridesmaid is the bride's sister, Mary Wright and next to her is the bride's mother. Behind the bride is her brother, George Wright junior and on his left, the father of the bride George Wright senior. Next to the groom is his mother Mrs Carter and second from the left on the back row is his father, Revd Christopher Carter. Other guests include Aunt Elizabeth Wright, William Wright and schoolmaster Mr D.G. Douglas.

STATE TRUMPETER. Mr George Wright senior, (1846-1937), at the turn of the century, in his uniform as one of the two men who were titled the Derbyshire State Trumpeters. Mr Wright was also a leading member of the Spondon Village Brass Band. They played in the leading escort carriage from Rowsley station to Chatsworth House when Edward VII visited the home of the Duke and Duchess of Devonshire.

WEDDING, OCTOBER 1923. The wedding of Miss Marjorie Randle to Mr James Barr took place at St Werburgh's church. Shown sitting in the garden of the bride's home, No. 6 Church Street, are the bride's parents, Mrs Mary Randle and Mr William Thomas Randle. Mr Barr was a senior accountant with British Celanese Ltd and his wife was for many years Secretary of the St Werburgh's Parochial Church Council.

WHITSUN WALK, c. 1917. The Whit Tuesday walk from Spondon to the grounds of Locko Park, about one and a half miles, was a great tradition and took place annually until the 1920s. This particular event includes children of the Sunday schools and adults from the two Methodist churches and the parish church. Led by the Scout Band (right), there were also a few of the patients from the Spondon House Auxiliary Hospital, in their 'army blues', sitting front right.

WHITSUN PARADE, c. 1935. The Spondon Scouts, re-formed in 1928 as the 66th Derby (1st Spondon; Mrs Drury-Lowe's Own), prepare to lead the Whit Sunday Parade with their drum and fife band. The parade is lining up in Sitwell Street for an event which no longer occurs. The shop seen on the left is now an opticians and the White Swan public house can be seen in the background.

Six
Spondon Residences

In addition to Locko, which has a history going back in various forms to the twelfth century, a number of fine houses were built in the village itself from the eighteenth century onwards, mainly by wealthy business and professional people from Derby. At least six of these have been demolished in the twentieth century, but some remain.

LOCKO PARK. The parkland and house of Locko Park are on the north side of Spondon, about a mile from the village. The house was rebuilt between 1725 and 1730 and purchased in 1747 by John Lowe from the Gilbert family. Small portions of the old house still remain, including the very fine chapel, the projecting section of the property on the left, which dates back to 1669. The house and gardens stand in approximately 300 acres of parkland, including a large lake and a fruit farm.

NINETEENTH CENTURY PROOF. This view of the house is titled Locko Hall, 1855. It shows the house as it is entered through the main gateway from the parkland into the forecourt and gardens, past a beautiful area of rhododendrons. The date proves that the foreground projecting section of the house and the tower were built by this time, although some publications have given it a date of around 1890.

LOCKO ENTRANCE ARCH. At the end of the drive through the park visitors to the hall itself come to this magnificent arch, flanked by two statues holding lamps. Through the arch can be seen the stone balustrade and urns which used to front the main part of the house. These have now been removed, giving an uninterrupted view across to the parkland and the lake in the distance, although the distant clock tower still remains.

LOCKO LAKE. In the parkland of Locko stands this ornamental lake. It has changed little over the years and this unusual view looking west, around 1920, is almost identical to that of today. The lake was constructed in the nineteenth century on what was previously boggy ground, a causeway being built to create a dam and also to give a more direct access to the house. A public bridleway passes the lake but the house is not open to the public.

INGLE NOOK. Mr and Mrs Lewty in the garden of Ingle Nook, Sitwell Street, in 1890. It still stands, although somewhat altered and converted into flats. Much of the large garden has now become an area of modern housing, although remembered by the name Ingle Close. The house was built in the mid-nineteenth century for Mr Lewty, who worked for the Midland Railway, based in Derby. It remained the property of the Lewty family for nearly one hundred years.

THE HOMESTEAD, c. 1920. Spondon village's only Grade I listed building, The Homestead, in its present form dates to around 1745, but is thought to be around thirty years earlier in parts. It was built for a local tanner, but lived in for many years by four generations of the Cade family, most of whom were doctors. The horse and foal in the foreground are grazing on what is now Willowcroft Road, on land owned by dairy farmer Mr Tom Lather.

THE HOMESTEAD, c. 1890. An unusual view showing the rear of the house, taken in 1890 from the garden of Ingle Nook, presumably from a tree or other vantage point. The wall in the foreground is that of the 'Twitchell' running between the grounds of The Homestead and Ingle Nook, from Sitwell Street to Potter Street. Of considerable interest is the now demolished timber-framed building in the foreground, probably a barn or similar structure dating before The Homestead was built in 1745.

BANKSIDE, SITWELL STREET, *c.* 1920. The field behind the dog is now the site of the houses at the top of Willowcroft Road. Behind is Bankside, for many years the home of Mr and Mrs Housley. Mr Housley ran his chemists shop from the house until his move in the 1960s to the later site in Sitwell Street. The house has now been demolished and new houses erected on the site. This photograph and the one opposite are two separate shots taken by Mrs Lather.

THE START OF WILLOWCROFT ROAD, *c.* 1922. The open view across the valley from The Homestead was soon to be spoilt by the cutting of Willowcroft Road and the construction of houses. Gradually the house building extended along the whole length of Willowcroft Road and the filling-in of the space between the village and the Nottingham Road to the south had commenced. No mechanised diggers or dumper trucks then, just a spade and a wheelbarrow and sufficient man-power. Note the pile of timber scaffold poles in the background.

DR THOMAS CADE, 1871. Dr Cade on the steps of The Homestead, where he lived with his wife Eliza and their four children from 1840 to 1894. He was a doctor of considerable reputation and the third of four generations of Cades to own the house. His parents were Dr James and Mrs Romana Cade and it was on the death of his father that Thomas purchased the property from his father's executors. Romana was the daughter of the famous Derby painter Joseph Wright.

THE STABLES. Although altered by the addition of the garage door in the 1950s, The Homestead stables are now Grade II listed so no additional external alterations will occur. It is thought that the stables date a little after the main house and a date of about 1800 is estimated. The upper room of the building was used by the Spondon Scouts in the 1930s as their meeting place and in its time has had a variety of other uses.

FALCON'S NEST. Built on the Nottingham Road, this house was within the parish boundary of Spondon but originally had a postal address of 'Borrowash'. When it was built, around 1860, it was part of the isolated hamlet of Borrow-wood, sometimes spelt Borough-wood, a name which goes back to the fourteenth century. In the latter part of its life the building became offices for a local business and was finally demolished in 1996.

SPONDON HALL, c. 1930. This late eighteenth century house built for the Wilmot family, was the one-time home of the Cox family, Derby lead suppliers. The last occupier was Sir Henry Fowler, a former Chief Engineer of the LMS Railway. After he left it remained empty for some years when it was purchased by the Derby Childrens' Hospital, but work never commenced because of the Second World War. It was requisitioned during the war as an Officer Training Centre and after a second period of disuse, was demolished in the late 1950s.

SPONDON HALL STABLES. This is all that remained of the coach house and stables prior to their demolition in the 1950s. The grounds of the hall were extensive, with a large variety of rare trees and shrubs, lawns and flower gardens and a tennis court. The last occupier was a very enthusiastic sportsman. Two housing areas and a by-pass now cover much of the estate.

Seven

Spondon at Work

Until the nineteenth century industry was unknown in Spondon, except for hand frame stocking knitting in the cottages of the workers. Some people were walking to work in Borrowash and Derby mills, but the arrival of the railway made a great difference. Towards the middle of the nineteenth century frame knitting and being a domestic servant made the greatest demand on the villagers, by its end more men worked for the railway at Derby than in any other trade.

HAYMAKING. Haymaking in the in the 1930s in 'Colour Works Field', which stood between the Derby Road and the Leech Neal Colour Works. The field was originally part of the medieval 'Derby' Field, one of the three of the village field system, and had been in constant use for agriculture for over 800 years. Traces of the 'ridge and furrow' workings were very evident. It is now the site of the Asda supermarket and car park.

THE WHARF, SPONDON, 1892. A watercolour painting by a member of the Lewty family of Ingle Nook, Sitwell Street. The Derby Canal was opened in 1796 and the 'wharf' consisted solely of a bay on the north side of the canal, just large enough for a horse drawn narrowboat to be turned around, or moored alongside for unloading. It was primarily used for the delivery of coal for use in the village of Spondon, and sited on the Derby side of the Station Road canal bridge. Traces of it can still be seen on the south side of the Moon Hotel.

OSBISTON FARM. Mowing hay on the farm in about 1938. In the background are the cooling towers of Spondon Power Station, then controlled by the Notts and Derby Power Co. Osbiston House still stands in Gravel Pit Lane and the farm stretched southwards towards the Nottingham Road, which runs north of the power station. Now the whole area is covered by houses, except for the A52 which follows the line of the hedge at the bottom of the field.

MR HERBERT OSBISTON. Delivering milk, he is outside the entrance to the cemetery in Stoney Lane. In the distance there are the houses of Moor Street. Around 1930, Stoney Lane was, as the name suggests, just an unmade road, although it was the main road from Spondon to Borrowash. Now the hedge and trees have all been removed to make way for houses and bungalows.

LEECH NEAL COLOUR WORKS, *c.* 1935. This view looks north east from the Derby Corporation sewage works, with the village of Spondon in the background. The extensive Leech Neal business, which prior to 1915 was Spondon's largest employer, finally closed down in the 1940s. Little of the colour works remains, most of the site being taken over by the huge A52 fly-over at the intersection with the city ring road, Raynesway. Beyond the trees and the hedge now stands an Asda superstore. Between the two chimneys is Merchant Avenue, houses built in the late 1920s, and on the hill behind is St Werburgh's church. The houses on the right were built by British Celanese.

FACTORY CHIMNEY. One of Leech Neal's chimneys had a distinct lean, with a slight bend at one point. Two lines have been drawn on the photograph to show the amount out of true. The chimney stood long after the factory closed and was finally demolished in the 1960s. The company finally sold out to a major chemicals company and the factory had a variety of uses, and is now the site of Albert Loomes Ltd, motor vehicle dismantlers.

OUT TO ENJOY THEMSELVES, c. 1924. Leech Neal for years had an annual outing, strictly for employees only, no wives or husbands, (if they employed married women). The destination is unknown; the group have been described as the 'cap and bowler brigade' with what appears to be 100 per cent with headgear. One of the few with a trilby is Mr George Wright senior, on the left of the third row, who is carrying his trumpet, probably to summon the group together again when it is time to return.

COMPANY OUTING, *c.* 1925. Approximately half the normal workforce of 200 is featured on the photograph, with just four ladies. With one exception every lady and gentleman is wearing a hat of some description. The venue of this outing is also unknown. It is believed that the four ladies in the picture were the only ladies employed on the Spondon site. Two of the ladies were industrial chemists, one was the company secretary and the fourth was the manager's secretary. For the company to employ female industrial chemists was quite unusual at this time.

COOLING TOWERS. For many years the cooling towers of Spondon Power Station dominated the sky line at the south east side of the village. Originally built by British Celanese to supply power to their factory, it was sold to the Notts and Derby Power Company in 1929, from whom it passed to the C.E.G.B. It became redundant and the towers were subsequently demolished. The dog is looking at the eyesore which spoils his view from the foundations of an old Spondon farm building.

THE RAYNESWAY BRIDGE. In 1938 the Borough of Derby opened a new section of ring road, the northern section of which crossed the River Derwent and entered into the south east corner of Spondon. The bridge over the river, which divided Spondon from Alvaston, suffered a disaster less than nine years later in 1947. Following the heavy snows and hard frost throughout Derbyshire came a rapid thaw, which caused the river to flood and erosion of the bank stressed the bridge. The centre pier collapsed and the bridge gave way. It was out of commission for some time before repair and strengthening work was completed.

THE STATION INN. In Station Road, the inn had been so named following the opening of Spondon station in 1839. It was already in existence before that date, called The Canal Tavern because of the canal which passed nearby. In the 1920s, men working at the nearby British Celanese factory would come off the morning shift at 2.00 pm and stop for a pint or two, many also eating their sandwiches. Because the closing times of the inn and later the Moon Hotel, coincided with the 2.00 pm and 10.00 pm shift change time, they had a special licence which allowed them to serve drinks for an extra ten minutes to shift workers only.

THE MOON HOTEL. By 1929 the Station Inn had been replaced on the same site by the more superior Moon Hotel. At shift-ending times thousands would pour over the level crossing adjacent to Spondon station and climb the canal bridge on their way home. It was impossible for any vehicles to proceed up or down Station Road at this time. If a train passed through the level crossing gates were closed and the only way forward was to cross the line by the congested footbridge.

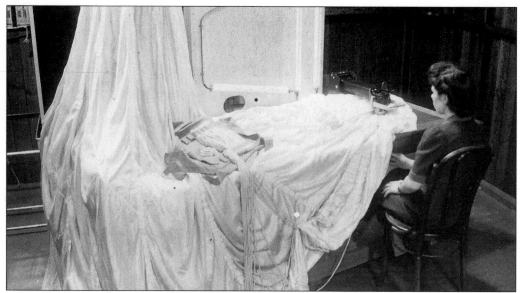

PARACHUTE MAKING. In 1916 a company which later become British Celanese Ltd, took over 360 acres of land at the southern edge of Spondon to manufacture a protective 'dope' for aircraft body fabric. In 1920 they started producing a synthetic yarn which was to became known worldwide as 'Celanese'. By 1940 they were manufacturing a huge variety of products to help the war effort. One of these was the manufacture of parachutes, the panels of which are here being sewn together.

PARACHUTE INSPECTION. The parachutes were minutely inspected for any flaws in the weaving of the material and the sewing of the panels. As can be seen by the lady inside the parachute, they were inspected both internally and externally. The majority of the parachutes were used for dropping supplies to ground forces, rather than as emergency 'chutes for airmen or members of the Parachute Brigade.

ENGINEERING WORKSHOP. The Central Engineering Department's main workshop, commonly known to all the employees as '29 Plant', in the 1940s. Due to the secret nature of much of the company's work, it was advisable to produce on site the majority of the components required for the many production machines. The machinists and other members of the engineering workshops were highly skilled, producing components, assemblies and fabrications of high quality.

YARN DYEHOUSE. The dyeing of yarn was a highly skilled operation, as the colours had to be consistent over a long period of time to ensure a perfect match with earlier and later batches. The colourists knew exactly how much of the appropriate dye had to be added to ensure the correct shade required, without the aid of the highly sophisticated equipment available today.

RIBBON WEAVING. A very smartly dressed young lady tends a row of ribbon weaving looms, again in the 1940s. Safety-minded persons of today would shudder at the thought of someone not wearing a regulation overall or head covering when working such equipment and it was not long after this period that stringent safety measures were introduced throughout the factory. Note the almost regulation painting of the rear wall, the lower 5 ft of green with cream above.

CURTAIN DISPLAY. Another of the Celanese products around 1947 was Celanet, for net curtains. Here is a warehouse mock-up of a display unit, with two young lady employees pressed into action as photographic models. Presumably the idea would then be used as a studio set for future major advertising. After the Second World War, a whole variety of new products were produced from the basic acetate yarn spun, woven or knitted on the Spondon site.

GALA DAY. From 1947 onwards British Celanese ran an annual field day, with athletics, shows, circus acts and the like for employees and their families. It usually included a display of the company's products and on one occasion, a mannequin parade, with young women from the factory modelling the latest gowns, garments and swimwear made from Celanese materials. This display of fabrics with an early 1930s theme was in a marquee in the 1948 event.

FACTORY SITE, *c.* 1925. This view is from the railway footbridge, some ten years after the start of the company. Two groups of men are gathered round the entrance, probably waiting to be interviewed for a job. Some of the early factory buildings are in the background and a couple of the old steam engines are towing goods round the site. Most of the transportation within the site was by flat railway trucks towed by these engines. Later employees will be surprised to see that the site is as yet unfenced.

LEAVING THE FACTORY, *c.* 1927. With only two exits, one at the Alvaston end of the site and the main one at the Spondon end, it was always going to be a mass exit at shift change times. By now the factory had been fenced and the boarding was retained until the 1950s, complete with the notice board. The horses and carts waiting to gain entrance were probably carrying building materials, as continued expansion brought about almost permanent building contractors on site.

STATION ROAD, 1940s. Hundreds leave the factory gate and walk up Station Road after the day shift ended at 6.00 pm. The station building and footbridge are on the left and the north end of the factory buildings is in the background. Many will remember Mr George Whiteman's newspaper kiosk which stood on the station side of the road, and Mr Wilson's confectionery and tobacco stall opposite.

THE STAFF BALL, 1950. In the late 1940s and early 1950s, the ball was held at the old Assembly Rooms, Derby, later demolished following a disastrous fire. The group enjoying the *Palais Glide* in 1950, from the left, include Molly Brown, an unnamed couple, Ashley Brown, Gwen Jackson, Mary Hughes, John Hughes, Vivien Brown and Alan Jackson. In the background can be seen three members of one of Derby's major dance bands, The Freddy Sharratt Orchestra. The Assembly Rooms, an eighteenth century structure, was always considered a rather up-market location for company and social similar occasions.

BRITISH CELANESE TABLE TENNIS CLUB, 1951/2. From the end of the Second World War until the company became part of the Courtaulds organization in 1957, British Celanese made efforts to encourage sporting activities for the employees. In 1947 a Table Tennis Club was formed and by 1951 it became a most popular and successful part of the company's sporting scene. The club was one of the largest in the Derby Association and a number of its players were members of the County or Derby teams. Members are, back row, from left to right: Alan Caughey, John Challis, Trevor Fox, Roger Foggan, Ben Whittaker, Dan Bland, Harold Cordery, Rex Wilcock, Harry Lowson, Theo Hoogerwerf, Mike Shaw, Ashley Brown. Centre row: Rose Hardy, -?-, -?-. Front row: Harold Holborn, Mrs Suniewski, John Hughes, Geoff. Browne, Janet Barker, Bill House, Betty Caughey and Mabel Roy.

Eight
Chaddesden

Chaddesden is also a village with a very old foundation. Listed in the Domesday Survey as 'Cedesdene' it had the high number of eleven freemen and a rateable value far above that of its neighbour Spondon. Its closeness to Derby brought about a great expansion in the late 1920s and into the 1930s, continuing in the '50s and '60s. This made it an obvious dormitory village for Derby and despite much opposition, the incorporation into the old Borough was inevitable. Little now remains of the old village except the part fourteenth century church and a few houses in the church area.

CHADDESDEN VILLAGE, c. 1930. The village, at the north end of Chaddesden Lane. On the immediate right is Church Lane, and the old house on the corner has now been demolished. The houses on the left still exist, with the village school hidden beyond them. This is almost all of the original village centre, with the short lane up to the church, a few cottages continuing beyond the distant bend into Morley Lane, a now demolished Methodist chapel in Brook Lane plus the hall and parkland.

VILLAGE COTTAGES, *c.* 1905. The old cottages stood at the rear of the former Chaddesden Post Office, in Morley Lane, near the house now called The Old Bakery. The post office and the cottages were sited on the east side of Morley Lane, between the existing Wilmott Garage and Chaddesden Brook. The brook is at the lowest point of the lane, passing underneath it, unknown to many new residents of the area.

TOWER VIEW, *c.* 1936. Looking north west from the tower of the Parish Church of St Mary. In the centre, middle distance, can be seen the greenhouses of a nursery which stretched from the village up to Chaddesden Park Road, the then new houses of which appear in the background. The greenhouses are on the location of what was to become Reginald Road South. The equally new houses of Max Road are on the extreme right middle distance.

CHADDESDEN HALL, *c.* 1920. The hall was built in about 1740 as a home for a branch of the Wilmot family and on the site of an earlier structure. It was demolished in the 1920s and removed so completely that few people are aware of its exact location. It was approached off Chaddesden Lane, south of the church and here the entrance from the lane can be seen. The parkland of the hall is now a public park.

HALL AND STABLES. A general view from Chaddesden Lane with the property fronted by a fairly high wall to discourage too many prying eyes, although the Wilmot family took much interest in the village and its activities. The approximate location of the hall is where Chaddesden Library now stands. The Wilmot family had held land in the area since 1539. The hall was extensively repaired and renovated in the 1840s.

THE HALL PARK. The park and lake were fed by Lee's Brook and the rear of the hall is in the background. The conservatory attached to the south east wing was a later addition, probably in the improvements of 1840 and does not seem to add to the overall appearance of the building. A writer in the mid-1800s described the land as being 'embowered with plantations and shrubberies'.

SIR HENRY WILMOT, Bart, KCB, VC. One-time owner and resident of Chaddesden Hall, who died in 1901, Sir Henry was a much respected land owner in the area. In 1904 a memorial to him, consisting of oak panelling and altar rails, was erected in Chaddesden Parish Church, from his various tenants in both Chaddesden and Spondon. His family presented a reredos of oak and alabaster at the same time.

VILLAGE FETE. It seems that the whole of Chaddesden turned out to help or participate in this event of 1917. This twenty-page programme includes a list of seventy-nine patrons, a programme of music by the Derby Town Prize and Sherwood Foresters Bands, and an unnamed dance band. There were competitions and stalls and a 'Great Walking Match' for 'Ladies and Soldiers (in full uniform)' each day from Derby Market Place to Chaddesden Hall, with first prizes valued at 30 shillings each.

Official Programme.

Old Village Fair and Revels,

In aid of Lord Roberts' Memorial Workshops for Wounded and Disabled Soldiers and Sailors,

CHADDESDEN HALL & GROUNDS,

AUGUST BANK HOLIDAY, AUGUST 6th,
TUESDAY, Aug 7th, WEDNESDAY, Aug. 8th.

To be opened on Monday by HIS WORSHIP THE MAYOR OF DERBY.

On Tuesday by the Deputy-Mayor, Mr. ALBERT GREEN.

On Wednesday by A. E. BECK, Esq.

Admission—2 to 5 p.m., **6d.**; 5 to 9 p.m., **3d.**

PROGRAMME ONE PENNY.

THE 27th DERBY SCOUT GROUP, c. 1915. Founded in 1912 by the Vicar of Chaddesden, the Revd Alliss-Smith, it has been in continuous existence since then, the oldest group in the district. The Vicar and the Scouts received much encouragement and support from Miss Constance Wilmot of Chaddesden Hall and the troop with the Vicar and Miss Wilmot are in front of the hall. The inset photographs are of absentee assistant leaders, Quarter-master Sergeant Newton (left), A.J. Evans (centre) and W.M. Collyer.

CHADDESDEN SCHOOL, *c.* 1912. Erected in 1872, the school was very soon found to be too small for the number of children in the village and so was enlarged in 1889 to accommodate a total of 100 children. It has now ceased to be used as a school and is the area's Community Centre. The school building seems to have changed little over the intervening years, but the surroundings have altered considerably, with houses on both sides and to the rear.

NOTTINGHAM ROAD. On 28 June 1906, Edward VII visited Derby, when he unveiled the memorial to Queen Victoria. His route also took him along the Nottingham Road, including the section approaching Chaddesden. Crowds are beginning to gather and the old Derby Co-op Warehouse is displaying its banner of welcome. The flags and bunting decorate the road into the distant Cemetery Hill.

CHADDESDEN PARK ROAD, *c.* 1922. This is the junction with Nottingham Road, when development of the area had just commenced, the whole area now being fully built over. Much has been added since this date, including footpaths, curbing, a normal road surface and full development along the entire length, which stretches over the hill in the distance. Last to be built over is the land in the foreground, which was completed only a few years ago.

CHADDESDEN LANE, *c.* 1937. Round the bend is the end of Chaddesden Lane, at its junction with Wilsthorpe Road, showing the relatively new shops on the corner. From this point the road becomes Morley Lane. The old commemoration tree, electricity control box and grassed area have now all given way to a much-altered layout, with a wider exit from Wilsthorpe Road and a footpath on both sides of the road.

LEES BROOK. The old bridge at the bottom of Chapel Lane, crossing Lees Brook and leading over to Brook Farm. It was later replaced by a less picturesque steel structure which is still standing. Lees Brook rises in Locko Park, Spondon, flows through Chaddesden and into the River Derwent south of the village. Extensive flood prevention work has eliminated much of the flooding which had plagued the village for hundreds of years.

CHAPEL LANE. Viewed from Brook Farm, looking up the lane, the chapel which gave the thoroughfare its name stood just beyond the bridge, on the left. It has been demolished for some years, having previously been converted into a dwelling, but the lane still retains some of its old character. The hedge on the right still exists, as do two cottages, possibly of eighteenth century origin. On the other side houses reflect the architecture of the 1930s right up to the 1990s.

BROOK FARMHOUSE, c. 1960. An old farm, the house formerly thatched, it was run by the Morten family for many years. It is one of the older farms of the village and like most of them, it concentrated on mixed arable and cereal crop production. In 1845 fifteen farms were listed in the village and by 1924 there were still eleven in production, but since that date much land has been taken over for housing.

BROOK FARMYARD. Looking at the same area today, few people would imagine the difference, the farm buildings having been converted to residential property. This section of the farm property stands at the side of the Lees Brook which gives the farm its name. Instead of a natural, wild, grassy bank, the brook, contained in a culvert, now has an immaculate lawn running to its edge.

CHADDESDEN GUIDES, 1980. For many years, the Chaddesden Carnival has continued to be a major attraction, not only in the immediate area, but visitors come from all of the area around. Various village organizations take part in the parade and events in the display ring at the park. There are also fairground items, carnival band displays and the like. The Guides decorated a lorry to publicise their 70th anniversary.

A PAGEANT OF GUIDING, 1980. The Guides' event in the park consisted of a short pageant showing the seventy years since the Guides first appeared at a Scout rally at the Crystal Palace, to put forward to Lord Baden-Powell their request for a separate organization for girls. Lord Baden-Powell asked his sister, Agnes, to form the Girl Guides and Mrs Molly Brown as Agnes Baden-Powell leads a group of Girl Scouts to start the first Guide Company.

Nine

Ockbrook

The village of Ockbrook is half of the combined parish of Ockbrook and Borrowash. Mentioned in the Domesday Book it was one of the estates of Geoffrey of Alselin, but it has a much earlier foundation. A little to the east of the present village the foundations of a farmhouse, pottery or similar building of the early Roman period has recently been excavated - all of great archaeological interest. It is the only example of its kind found in the southern half of Derbyshire. In Victorian times it became well known for the manufacture of silk stockings, many cottagers working hand looms, and they even supplied Queen Victoria. Now manufacturing of any type has virtually ceased and the population mainly works in Derby, Spondon, or Ilkeston.

OCKBROOK c. 1904. This is almost the whole of the village as it existed nearly one hundred years ago, from Red Hills on the east side of the village and the path to nearby Hopwell. Only the spire of the parish church can be seen above the trees on the left and in the middle distance on the right is the three storey high Ockbrook House. At the top of the distant slope on the right is part of the Moravian Settlement.

ALL SAINTS, OCKBROOK.

THE PARISH CHURCH. The present structure of All Saints' church is a mixture of various ages, with the tower dating to the second half of the twelfth century and the spire 150 years later. Various additions were made over the centuries, including a sixteenth century screen, a nineteenth century font and an 1835 enlargement. Although the Domesday Survey makes no mention of a church at Ockbrook, there is also a font of Anglo-Saxon design.

Borrowash.
All Saints' Church, Ockbrook.

CHURCH STREET. Although the twin villages of Ockbrook and Borrowash share a joint parish council, it is unlikely that the residents of the older village of Ockbrook were very favourable towards the producer of this particular view of their church, which was headed 'Borrowash'. Dated around 1910, it also shows the White Swan Public House on the left and the houses beyond, in a view which is almost the same today.

COLE LANE, *c.* 1920. This view shows the lane before any houses were built on the left side until Collier Lane, at the bottom of the hill. There were a few houses on the right, hidden by the trees and the hedges. At the top of the hill Carr Hill Farm is still a working farm which was run until recently by three generations of the Naylor family in turn. Ockbrook Parish Church lies at the bottom of the hill, where the lane continues into Church Street.

BARE LANE, *c.* 1910. The top of Bare Lane, with the lane going off on the right leading through the Moravian Settlement. The house up the lane which can just be seen through the trees still stands, but both lanes are now somewhat wider to take the increase in road traffic. The thatched farm outbuildings on the left have been demolished and the farmyard site is now the location of a petrol station, garage and haulage contractors.

BARE LANE, *c.* 1920. Looking up the lane in the opposite direction, the scene hardly gives the impression that it is quite a steep hill. The farmhouse on the right is part of the farm mentioned on the preceding page. Both sides of the lane are now lined with houses. The gate on the right is approximately where Pares Way now commences and large new houses stretch up the road on the left. At the top on the left are some of the early Settlement houses.

VICTORIA AVENUE, *c.* 1902. The main road connecting Borrowash to Ockbrook, looking down on the whole of Ockbrook. The Queen's Head public house is in the distance on the left side and beyond it, the old forge. The house at the bottom of the hill, behind the wagons, still stands at the corner of Collier Lane. Houses have now been built along both sides of the avenue, except on the cricket field from the bottom of the hill to the Queen's Head.

VICTORIA AVENUE, *c.* 1925. Viewed from almost the same position as the previous photograph, the right side is still partially undeveloped. The two villages are now split by the Borrowash By-pass, part of the A52 from Derby to Nottingham. A road bridge over the by-pass now joins the Ockbrook to the Borrowash sections of the avenue, which contains some very fine houses built from the early Victorian period onwards.

THE MORAVIAN SETTLEMENT, *c.* 1902. In the mid-eighteenth century the Moravians built a settlement at Ockbrook, on land donated to them. It allowed them to follow their own ideas of non-conformism and at first the locals were rather disturbed by their presence. The church is on the left and by the beginning of the nineteenth century, a girls' boarding school had been established in the late eighteenth century building to the right, now the Head's house and Liley House.

SCHOOL AND CHURCH, *c.* 1950. The Settlement, showing the main school buildings left and centre, the Manse centre front and the church with its distinctive cupola bell-housing next to it. The church was built in 1752 but the bell-tower was a later addition and the clock was installed in 1827. The buildings have changed little over the last one hundred years and are all about two hundred years old.

'THE GRANGE' *c.* 1954. The Ockbrook Moravian Girls School Senior House in the 1950s, is now used for general school purposes and known as 'The Grange'. A fine example of a mid-Victorian gentleman's residence, it was originally called the Swallows Rest. Beyond the house, left, can be seen the gable end of The Mount, another house of similar age and now used for the school's junior section.

A STATELY SETTING. In 1920, before being purchased by the Moravian Girls School, it was for two or three years the home of Lord Petersham, later to become the tenth Earl of Harrington. The ancestral home of the Earls of Harrington is in the nearby village of Elvaston. The eleventh Earl was born in the house. It had originally been built for a former head of the Moravian Boys School, which ceased to exist during the First World War.

THE GARDEN. The beautiful setting of the terraced garden of 'The Grange' has been a feature of the Girls School since the 1950s, although the gardens were set out many years earlier. This view looks down the drive to the road of the Settlement and on, across Ockbrook to the fields and hills beyond. The lawns were the scene of the annual school fete, which the writer can remember attending for several years in succession.

SECOND YEAR JUNIORS. The girls (and one boy) of a junior school form, in the grounds of The Mount. I am not stating the year but the group includes my own daughter. One obvious point is the capacious pockets of the school dresses, which seemed to carry everything a young girl may need, or in at least one case, did not need, as one of them was known to slip any unwanted pieces of school lunch into them.

THE LECTURE HALL, *c.* 1930. The road through the Settlement as it nears the top of Bakehouse Lane. The Lecture Hall is on the left and adjoins a house called Greenside. Both were requisitioned in the First World War for use as an Auxiliary Hospital. The Lecture Hall is now used for a variety of purposes, including, as the name suggests, lectures. On the right is the Lodge, one-time lodge-house for The Grange.

BAKEHOUSE LANE, *c.* 1925. The approach to the Moravian Settlement, from Flood Street. As the name suggests, it once housed the Moravian's bakehouse. The fields on both sides of the lane were subsequently developed in the 1970s and the land now contains houses. The building on the extreme right is The Mount and the single storey building in the centre is the Grange Lodge. To the right is the rear of the Lecture Hall and Greenside House.

THE OLD COTTAGES, *c.* 1900. These cottages stood on the eastern edge of the Settlement, but had been in that location long before the Settlement was even considered. By 1900 they had become very dilapidated and as can be seen here, the thatch was beginning to drop off. They gradually deteriorated until the only answer was to demolish them. These days they would probably fetch a high price as 'in need of some renovation'.

VILLAGE BROWNIES. The 1st and 2nd Ockbrook Brownie Packs at a garden party at the home of Mr and Mrs Horton in 1952. It was held to raise funds for a joint pack holiday. The 1st Ockbrook Pack were from Ockbrook Girls School, and the 2nd Ockbrook Brownies were made up of girls who were residents of the village, meeting in the village Guide HQ. All were founded, along with the two Ockbrook Guide Companies, in the mid-1920s by Miss Mabel Nelson of Ockbrook. Back row, from left to right: Mrs B. Stanley and Mrs M. Hughes, (Brownie Leaders), Mrs M. Jackson, Miss G. Nichols, (District Guide Commissioner), Mr C. Addey, Mrs Horton, Mr Horton and Mrs Kennedy (Guide Captain). Among the Brownies were Valerie Frost, Margaret Wesson, Fiona Jackson, Christina Hunter and Cherry Jackson, of the 1st Ockbrook Pack. The 2nd Ockbrook Pack included Joan Slater, Jean Stevens and Margaret Coopey.

Ten

Borrowash

A separate village on the north bank of the River Derwent, but part of the combined parish of Ockbrook and Borrowash, the village was basically formed north of both the river and its early cotton mill. With the coming of the canal and later the railway, plus its location on the main turnpike road from Derby to Nottingham, it grew from the eighteenth century onwards. It has an earlier history, as there are records of the monastery at Dale owning a water-driven corn mill in the fifteenth century. In the early nineteenth century the Noak's Ark public house was the receiving point for the mails destined for Ockbrook, Spondon, Chaddesden and Elvaston.

NOTTINGHAM ROAD, c. 1905. This is the junction with Derby Road and Victoria Avenue - on the right behind the Forester's Arms public house. The properties on the left and in Derby Road (ahead) are still standing, but the public house and the post office, on the extreme right, have been demolished. This right corner is now the site of a supermarket car park. The gap between the shops on the left has now been filled by two shops and, like those on either side, with living facilities above.

VICTORIA AVENUE, c. 1930. This part of the Borrowash section is almost unrecognisable today. The A52 by-pass cuts off the road just beyond the two houses visible on the right. A new section veers off right and over a bridge to join the Ockbrook section beyond the by-pass. The first house on the left is now a medical centre and the wall has been demolished to give access to the new Greenway Close.

NOTTINGHAM ROAD, c. 1903. Looking towards Draycott and Nottingham, the first house on the left is now the post office. The open land on the left side of the road was then the property of Barron's Nurseries. When the Forester's Arms was demolished about twenty years ago, the licence and name were transferred to new premises just before the bend in the distance. Nottingham Road follows the line of the old Roman Road which ran from Derby to the River Trent near Sawley.

MISS LOTTIE RICE, *c.* 1900. A studio portrait of Miss Rice of Broughton House, in costume for a fancy dress party. Miss Rice was for many years a teacher at Spondon. The portrait was taken by Frederick J. Boyes of Derby, who announced that he had an 'electric and daylight studio'. Even after her marriage to Mr S.C. Nichols, she insisted on being 'Miss Rice' to her pupils.

CHRISTMAS, 1904. A very sober-looking Edwardian Christmas card from the Rice family of Broughton House, which is on the main Nottingham Road, Borrowash. The card was sent by Miss Rice to Mr S.C. Nichols, her future husband. Broughton House stands on the south side of Nottingham Road, almost opposite the present post office. At the time of the Rice family, it was almost on the edge of the main village.

THE NICHOLS FAMILY. Mrs Nichols (née Rice) with her daughter Gwenyth and a cousin of Gwenyth's in about 1924. Gwenyth became very well known in Spondon and Chaddesden, both for her work with the Guide Movement and as an amateur photographer. She ran the Spondon Flight Air Rangers, was the District Commissioner for Guides for the Derby East District and later, Division Commissioner for Derby. Her photographic work gained her many awards as a member of the British Celanese Camera Club.

WILLIAM BARRON & SON LTD'S NURSERY, c. 1920. William Barron was the famous head gardener at Elvaston Castle. The nursery extended over a large area on the east side of the village. At this time they appear to be one of only four businesses in Borrowash with a telephone. The site of the nursery is now covered by a privately developed housing estate, but the name and business is perpetuated by Barron's Way, Rose Avenue and Briar Close.

GORDON ROAD. This is a road of fairly large late Victorian houses, running south from the main Derby to Nottingham Road. At the north end, on the main road, can be seen the Wesleyan Methodist church, built in 1825. Most of the residents of the road were either senior employees at the nearby cotton or hosiery mills, or worked in Derby, taking the train from Borrowash station.

BORROWASH STATION, c. 1900. Viewed from the railway bridge in Station Road, looking towards Derby, the first station was opened in 1839 when the Nottingham to Derby line came into operation. This station soon followed, with a loading bay onto which carriages could be directly backed, which served the Earl of Harrington from Elvaston. In those early days people with horse drawn carriages were able to have them transported by rail when they were on long journeys, complete with a truck for the horses if required.

THE 'TOP LOCK'. Borrowash 'Top Lock' is now an area of open land, part of a footpath from Spondon to Borrowash. The Derby Canal was filled in around 1970 although it had not been used commercially since 1940. By the 1950s the canal had silted up and the wooden building on the right was bulldozed directly into the remains of the lock. The scene is looking towards Spondon about half a mile west of Borrowash station. The River Derwent, the canal and the railway run almost side-by-side.

THE RIVER DERWENT, c. 1905. This is not a typical scene as it appears to show the river in flood, with water well over the normal banks. It was not unusual for the river to flood in this area, but due to flood prevention schemes carried out in the '20s and '30s there has been some easing of the problem, although not total elimination. The weir was originally constructed to enable a water wheel to power machinery at a cotton mill.

Eleven
Elvaston, Thulston, Alvaston Shardlow and Wilne

Elvaston and Thulston are small non-industrial villages south of Borrowash and on the opposite side of the River Derwent. Both are centred around the former estate of the Stanhopes, later to become the Earls of Harrington. The two villages are separated by only one field, Elvaston containing the church, and Thulston the village pub. Alvaston, on the other hand, lies iummediately to the east and although a village for over 1,000 years, is now part of the City of Derby. It is both industrial and residential. Alvaston shares most of its northern boundary, the River Derwent, with Spondon and Chaddesden. Shardlow and Great Wilne is one parish but again separate villages. Prior to 1950s boundary changes, Shardlow gave its name to the Rural District which covered all the villages in this book.

ELVASTON CASTLE c. 1830. The hall, the former seat of the Earls of Harrington, was partly rebuilt in 1817 with the east wing remaining from the earlier 1633 house. Finances prevented the third Earl from completing the wing before his death in 1829. It was never completed to the original design, but in 1837 the fourth Earl went ahead with work incorporating the earlier brickwork and floor levels. The roof level was castellated and the completed building given the title of Elvaston Castle.

ELVASTON CASTLE GARDENS. 10.

E. MARTIN
(COPYRIGHT)

CASTLE GARDENS, *c.* 1908. The gardens at Elvaston Castle became famous from the middle of the nineteenth century, when William Barron was employed as head gardener by the fourth Earl of Harrington. William worked for the Earl from 1830 until the Earl's death in 1850, by which time the gardens had become one of the most outstanding in the country. The fifth Earl opened the gardens to visitors and Barron started to sell trees, mainly conifers, for which he was well known.

THE NINTH EARL. The Earl receives a trophy in connection with his position as the Master of the South Notts Hunt. He is pictured outside Elvaston Castle in about 1927. He was a well loved man, affectionately known as 'Old Whiskers'. His death in 1928 at the age of 69 caused much mourning and he was a keen follower of hounds almost until his death.

ST BARTHOLEMEW'S CHURCH. Sited in Elvaston Park near the Castle, it was rebuilt in the latter half of the fifteenth century and has some details of an earlier church. There are several memorials to the Stanhope family who were elevated to the Peerage to become the Earls of Harrington. In 1643 Sir John Gell, the Parliamentary Governor of Derby, attacked the hall and church in a personal attack on the Stanhope family. He entered the church and defaced the memorial to Sir John Stanhope.

CASTLE STABLES AND CHURCH, c. 1920. Immediately ahead is the stable block, part of the early nineteenth century rebuilding of the hall. In front of the main block is a cobbled yard, with extensive stables on each side for the coach horses and hunters. Through the arch was the coach yard and kennel yard for the hounds. All this is now freely open as part of the Elvaston Country Park. In the right foreground is Home Farm, now a farming museum.

THE 'GOLDEN GATES', *c.* 1904. The Castle's famous gates were obtained from a palace in Madrid in the mid-eighteenth century by the fourth Earl of Harrington. They formed the 'inner gates' from the former London Road entrance. As the entrance to the park, now a County Council country park, is at the opposite end of the estate, the majority of visitors never walk right through the gardens to see this fine example of wrought ironwork.

THULSTON, *c.* 1905. This is Elvaston's near neighbour and also originally part of the Harrington Estate. The Harrington Arms Inn on the extreme left and the farmhouse, centre, still stand as the centre of the village. The road facing leads to Elvaston, a quarter of a mile away. The houses in the middle distance have now been replaced and instead of the road turning to the right in front of the farm, it now turns almost in front of the camera position.

ST MICHAEL'S, ALVASTON. The church was entirely rebuilt in 1855, so this scene, from around 1900, shows a comparatively new building. A church was mentioned in the Domesday Survey of 1086 and items from an early English church were found in the foundations of the old tower when it was demolished. Many of the old monuments were replaced after the rebuilding. The thatched cottages to the right have now been demolished, the road widened and new houses have been built in the last twenty-five years.

THE LONDON ROAD, c. 1905. Originally a turnpike road, it led to a ferry over the River Trent near Shardlow. When the Cavendish Bridge replaced the ferry in 1771 it became the main road to London. Prior to this date, the road to the capital was via the Swarkestone Bridge, the most southerly point held by the forces of 'Bonnie Prince Charlie' in his ill-fated venture into England. The London Road is now the A6 linking the Derby City Centre to the south east.

THE TOLL HOUSE, *c.* 1902. When the tollpike road from Shardlow through to Derby was built, a toll house was erected at Alvaston, near to the site which has now become Alvaston Lake and Recreation Ground. It probably dates to the early 1800s. By the 1960s it had reached a very dilapidated state, was disused and in danger of demolition. It became a listed building and was then restored, and is still standing alongside the London Road footpath, as it was in 1902.

ALVASTON LAKE, *c.* 1930. The boating lake in Alvaston Park was built on the site of an old refuse tip in the late 1920s by Derby Corporation as a project to help relieve unemployment. The lake was fed by a stream which ran into the River Derwent, about 200 yards beyond the right of the picture. It was an extremely popular spot in the early 1930s, as can be seen by the variety of boats for hire.

ALVASTON LAKE, *c.* 1950. A similar location to the previous picture but by 1950 more flower beds had been planted and facilities had improved. Despite the lack of people, it had remained a very popular place. The house, built in the 1930s, was a tea room and home for a resident keeper. The lake was also very popular with local fishermen.

SHARDLOW HALL, *c.* 1900. This was built in 1684 by Leonard Fosbrooke, a man who had made his money by controlling all the river trade up-river from Nottingham. At that time the main road to the Wilden Ferry, a short way from the later Cavendish Bridge, took a large arc from the Dog and Duck Inn and went via Great Wilne. The present view of the hall is actually a rear view, the frontage being on the old road.

SHARDLOW HALL, *c.* 1910. The existing London Road was made in 1738, passing between the church and the hall. The property was purchased by a boat builder and canal carrier, James Sutton, who is listed as the owner in 1845. In the 1920s the house was used for some years as a preparatory school, but later became a research centre for the Ministry of Agriculture and Fisheries. The property was finally purchased in the 1980s by British Midlands Airways, who use it as the headquarters of their Accounts Department.

ST JAMES' CHURCH, *c.* 1902. Although of a much earlier style, the church was built in 1838 at a cost of approximately £6,000, which was raised locally. The only two changes apparent today are the loss of the pinnacles on the tower and the removal of the ivy from the chancel walls. This view from the east is from the adjacent field, which still exists. The London Road is off the picture to the right, running between the church and Shardlow Hall.

CAVENDISH BRIDGE, *c.* 1920. The bridge on the London Road, demolished by the flooding of the River Trent in 1947, was built in 1771 for over £3,000. It took the family name of the Dukes of Devonshire because a large proportion of the cost was born by the fourth Duke. On the extreme left is the old toll house, also now demolished, although the stone plaque showing the list of charges for passage over the bridge still exists by the side of the new bridge.

GREAT WILNE, *c.* 1914. Almost at the end of the road through the village, which continues as a track and ends at the footbridge over the River Derwent, the scene is little changed today, with the half-timbered house still standing alongside the field. In the distance the road continues in the direction of Shardlow, with the opening on the immediate right leading to a large farm building.

WILNE FOOTBRIDGE. Wilne stands on both sides of the River Derwent, near its confluence with the River Trent. The area on this side of the Derwent is Great Wilne or Far Wilne, usually listed alongside Shardlow, and part of that parish. The footbridge joined the two halves of Wilne, Church Wilne being on the far bank. The bridge has now been replaced by one of a more substantial construction, although somewhat less picturesque, approximately 200 metres downstream.

ST CHAD, CHURCH WILNE, c. 1908. Church Wilne lies on the northern side of the River Derwent, but very few people live in the village, primarily because much of it stands in the flood plain of the Rivers Derwent and Trent. Until recently the parish also included the larger nearby village of Draycott. The church dates in parts to the thirteenth and fourteenth centuries. In a disastrous fire of 1917, the roof and much of the interior was destroyed, but it was thoroughly restored in 1923.

Twelve
Dale Abbey,
Stanley and Morley

The three villages all have connections with each other, sharing joint boundaries and also adjoining the boundary of Spondon. Dale Abbey up to the time of the Dissolution in 1538 owned land in Stanley, and a farmhouse of theirs still exists in the village. It also held property at Borrowash and Spondon. Their lands spread far and wide and in the fields which divide the village of Dale Abbey from Ockbrook are said to be foundations of some abbey farm buildings. Morley church also contains various materials from the abbey. Until the nineteenth century, Stanley church was a chapelry of Spondon, although the building is older in parts than St Werburgh's at Spondon.

Hermits Cave, Dale, near Ilkeston

DALE ABBEY HERMITAGE. On the Ockbrook side of the village is the Hermit's Cave, carved out of the face of a sandstone cliff at the beginning of the twelfth century. According to legend, it was the home of a baker from Derby, who was told in a vision to go to a place called 'Depedale' and there live a life of solitude and religious service. The cave still exists and has stood the passage of time remarkably well.

Dale Abbey Ruins.

THE ABBEY. Impressed by the piety of the hermit, the Lord of the Manor gave land for the foundation of an abbey by the Augustinians. After initial problems and three failures, the Premonstratensian Order succeeded in about 1200 and the abbey became an important power in the area. At the Dissolution of the Monasteries in 1538 the abbot and monks were pensioned off and the abbey fell into ruin. Portions of it remain on the original site and in several buildings in the village.

Dale Abbey Ruins and Church. Nr. Ilkeston

ABBEY EAST WINDOW. The east window is the most prominent part of the abbey and is the one section which stands out to visitors above the surrounding houses as they enter the village. A private museum on the site holds some items which have been unearthed following excavations. In the distance is the old village church, and in the hillside beyond is the site of the hermit's cave.

DALE ABBEY CHURCH AND FARMHOUSE, *c.* 1905. This is a unique building in that the church only comprises half the structure, the other half being a farmhouse. The building is timber-framed and the farmhouse in its time has been an inn and was thought to have originally been the guest house or infirmary for the abbey. Internally the church has some rare and original wall paintings, a fifteenth century font and a large wooden gallery. It is still the church for Dale Abbey village and regular services take place.

DALE ABBEY VILLAGE, *c.* 1900. 'The Village' is the name of the road to the church and it is as quiet today as it appeared to be one hundred years ago. On the other side of the first building on the left, Manor House and Abbey House, is a portion of the abbey wall, now part of Abbey House itself. The white cottage on the bend of the road still looks almost the same today.

ST MATTHEW'S, MORLEY, c. 1912. The main part of the church dates back to early Norman times, with the north aisle rebuilt in the sixteenth century especially to house stained glass and other items from the dissolved monastery at Dale Abbey. Portions of the stained glass and some floor tiles can still be seen. Little has changed in the well wooded churchyard over the last ninety years.

CHURCH INTERIOR. The chancel of St Matthew's, in about 1915. The church is well known locally for the beauty and variety of the stained glass, of which the east window, dedicated to a member of the Bateman family, is considered to be the finest. Both nave and chancel contain memorials to many of the squires and other major residents of the village, including John Statham, who died in 1453, plus the Babbingtons, Sacheveralls and Sitwells.

THE MORLEY RECTORY. The very imposing rectory was built in the eighteenth century, with extensive alterations in the 1840s. It was too large for a modern incumbent to use and has been converted into a Diocesan Conference Centre and Retreat House, since when it has become a very busy place for diocesan and other activities. Nearby is the old timber-framed tythe barn.

THE STANLEY TRAMWAY. Built in the late nineteenth century to transport coal from the Stanley footrill (drift) mine, it was in operation until 1917, when the mine ceased to be viable. The colliery built a cable operated system on an inclined track from Stanley to Nottingham Road, Chaddesden, via the area now known as Oakwood. Colliers who lived in Chaddesden used to ride on the wagons, but as this was considered dangerous, special trucks were eventually built.

STANLEY SCOUT CAMP. In 1951 an international Scout camp, (the 7th World Jamboree) was held in Austria. A small group of boys from overseas were invited back to England, to camp at Stanley, by the Stanley Scouts. On their last evening in camp some of the ladies in the village decided to cook the boys a special meal. When the occasion arose, it appears that the number of volunteers considerably exceeded the number of boys, especially from the younger ladies.

STANLEY METHODIST CHAPEL CENTENARY. In 1961 the Methodists celebrated the centenary of the present Methodist chapel, although one had existed earlier. The Sunday school teachers on this special occasion were, standing, from left to right: Michael Green, Freda Severn, Roy Henstock, Edith Bull (now Mrs Green, wife of Paul) and Paul Green. Seated: Ruben Hemstock (father of Roy), Harry Green, (Superintendent and father of Paul and Michael) and Alec Winfield.

Thirteen

Breadsall and Little Eaton

The village of Breadsall is another of ancient foundation, north of Chaddesden. It was mainly agricultural, and the village itself is still surrounded by fields, although to the south it adjoins the Derby City boundary at Oakwood and Chaddesden. Little Eaton is sited in the valley along which runs the old Derby to Alfreton Road and Bottle Brook. It stands on limestone and in 1846 nine quarries were working, but by 1900 almost all had ceased operation.

BREADSALL, c. 1905. This is the centre of the village, with the old thatched cottage which later became Breadsall Post Office. The building still stands, although no longer the post office, and the thatch has been replaced by tiles. The road to Breadsall Priory and moor continues past the left of the church, taking the old line of the Roman Ryknield Street. Hidden behind the cottage is the Old Hall.

THE OLD HALL. It is of fourteenth century origin and was originally one of the two manors of Breadsall, but over the years much of it has been demolished. Since this print of 1869 was made the end wall has been taken down and the steps are on the outside of the building, leading across to an entrance on the new outer wall. Over the centuries it has been the rectory, joiners shop, school, inn, village shop, post office and now the Parish Room.

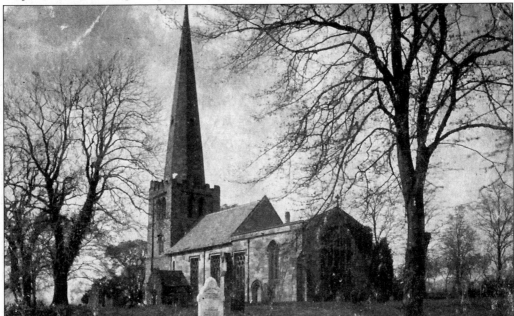

THE CHURCH BURNT OUT. The fire which so severely damaged the church occurred on 4 June 1914. After an extensive rebuilding programme, it reopened on 14 April 1916. All the interior woodwork was destroyed, the roof collapsed and the majority of the church stained glass and ornaments were lost or damaged. A small collection of rare chained books was also lost in the blaze. Many claim that suffragettes were to blame, but this has never been proved.

LITTLE EATON VILLAGE, *c*. 1900. A village street showing the typical limestone grey houses, which perch on the hillside, mainly to the west of the valley. All these older houses were built of the local limestone which was quarried from the hillside around. It is perhaps incorrect to call it a village, as the centre is officially named The Town. It was the end of a branch of the Derby Canal, completed in 1797, which carried local stone and coal from the Denby collieries.

THE ALFRETON ROAD, LITTLE EATON, *c*. 1920. Originally the main road, it was superseded by an early by-pass and again later by the A38. No-one now passing through the village would use it to go to Alfreton, but it does serve many of the newer houses on the west bank, then going on to the nearby village of Coxbench or turning back on to the early by-pass. The bridge is known locally as the 'Jack-o-Darley', crossing both the railway line and the Bottle Brook.

OLD ALICE, *c.* 1925. She lived with her parents in Little Eaton, but when they died, she refused to pay the cottage rent and was evicted by the landlord. She eventually found a spot in an old quarry where she lived in an old crate, with two boxes for her meagre belongings. She always kept a penny in her pocket, so that she could not be arrested for vagrancy. Curious visitors threw the odd copper but in the end she died in Shardlow Workhouse.

DRUM HILL, *c.* 1908. The hill stands directly east overlooking Little Eaton and over a hundred years ago was a busy quarrying site. Now only traces of the quarry remain and much of it is thickly wooded, mainly with silver birch. The footpath still exists, although a little wider than eighty years ago. The word 'Drum' in this context is derived from a Celtic word for knoll, so the name probably predates 500 AD and the Anglo-Saxon invasions.

DERBYSHIRE COUNTY SCOUT GROUP CAMP SITE. This stands on the top of Drum Hill and although not then an official camp site, there are records of Scouts camping there in 1918. By 1927 the site became official and in 1932 the Rovers of the Derby area built their own hut there. The stonework stood the test of time but the building was unfortunately burnt down some years ago.

LIFE ON 'THE HILL'. A weekend at Drum Hill, or 'The Hill' as it is generally known amongst Scouts and leaders from Derbyshire and other parts of the country, is always considered an event to remember. David Brown of Chaddesden in his Rover Scouting days of the mid-1950s, is apparently demonstrating how not to pour a dixie of boiling water into a mug, during one such weekend.

EARLY CAMPERS. As early as 1918 there are records of Scouts camping at Little Eaton Woods and it became a popular area for Derby Scout Troops. The Derby Post Office Troop was formed of boys from all over the area, working as telegraph boys from the age of thirteen. The Post Office obviously considered Scouting as a form of training to be encouraged. The boys are here seen in camp with their leader, Mr Dixon.